Skin Investigation

Brigitte Pace

Beauty Therapy Tutor IA (UK)

Table of Contents

Chapter 1

We all visit salons and spas at some point in our lives, whether it is for a simple manicure, waxing, facials or other treatment we fancy.

The truth is, most of us are unaware of what the awarded diplomas and certificates displayed mean and we take it for granted that the therapist knows how to do the job.

Let's take a deep look at the pros and cons when we accidentally bump into negligent therapists and the outcome it can have on clients.

Our health plays a very important part to having beauty treatments.

Most clients are completely do not realize that qualified therapists are bound by certain ethics. They are not allowed to treat clients who have health problems unless treatment is approved by a medical practitioner.

How many times have clients booked treatments, turned up and were treated only to return home and find out that an unexpected reaction took place?

Did you know that a simple carcinoma looks like a small pimple?

How many of us are aware of that?

During a facial treatment the circulation of the skin is increased, hence the redness in the area, and this is definitely not good for anyone who has a basal cell carcinoma.

And......... what about Acne?

Acne

A doctor prescribes medicine to clear up the infection and therapists will try and tell customers that their products work better.

Customers need to be aware of what is happening and how to recognize professionals in the Industry.

Not only is this becoming the norm nowadays, this is the kind of negligence that can cause harm and injury to clients.

Tell me, have you ever had a makeup in a salon?

Were the sponges clean?

Did the therapist sharpen the eyeliner pencil and lip pencil before you walked in?

Can you be sure that an eyeliner was not used on another client and then on you?

Did you ever go home and wake up the following morning with conjunctivitis?

What about those perfect eyebrow wax treatments which include tinting?

How many times do salon 'professionals' 'forget' to tint first and wax/tweeze hairs after tinting?

Did they forget or are they just plain careless!

4

Why you may ask?

The answer is simple. If waxing is done before tinting, the tint will penetrate into the open pores from the waxing and cause skin irritation and or/infection.

When you are treated by a professional this is what to expect

1. A proper consultation.
2. Excellent customer care.
3. Treatments that show results!

What is a Consultation Card..

Pets _____

First _____ Last _____

First _____ Last _____

Family Members _____

Address _____

Emergency Contacts

Pets Ah _____

1 Name: ☐Key   Email: _____

Location: Email: _____

Relationship: Home: _____ Work: _____

Home: Other: _____

Work: Directions: _____

2 Name: ☐Key

Phone:

Relationship:

Vet:

And... why is it important?

The consultation card provides the therapist with the client's personal details.

The Client's full name, contact number(s) the address. E-mail.

The next step during the consultation is to check for any major contra- indications to any treatment.

This part of the consultation is in fact the ultimate challenge for any Therapist since it will determine if the therapist has the ability to answer the client accurately about any contra-indication and why a particular treatment may not be suitable for the Client.

Our Skin!

The skin is the largest organ of the body, with a total area of about 20 square feet.

The skin protects us from microbes and the elements, helps regulate body temperature and permits the sensations of touch, heat, and cold.

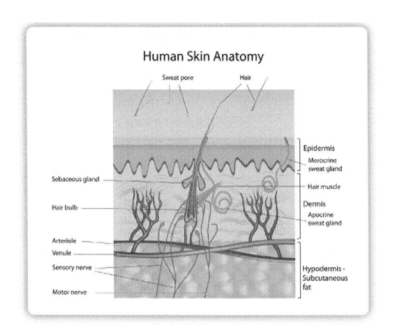

Human Skin Anatomy

Sweat pore   Hair

Epidermis
Merocrine sweat gland

Sebaceous gland

Hair muscle

Dermis
Apocrine sweat gland

Hair bulb

Arteriole
Venule

Sensory nerve

Motor nerve

Hypodermis - Subcutaneous fat

Skin Anatomy

The Skin is made up of three layers:

The epidermis, the outermost layer of the skin, provides a waterproof barrier and creates our skin tone.

The dermis, beneath the epidermis, contains tough connective tissue, hair follicles, and sweat glands.

The deeper subcutaneous tissue is known as the hypodermis. It is mainly made up of fat cells and connective tissue.

The skin's color is created by special cells called melanocytes, which produce the pigment melanin. These melanocytes are located in the epidermis.

Definitions of known Skin Conditions

Rash: Nearly any change in the skin's appearance can be called a rash.

Most rashes are from simple skin irritation; others result from medical conditions.

Dermatitis: A general term for inflammation of the skin.

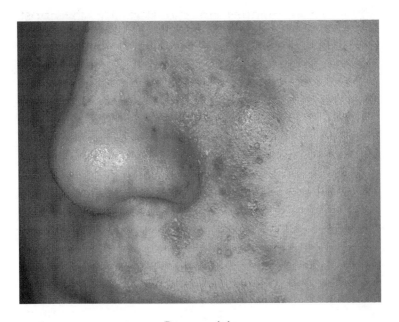

Dermatitis

Atopic dermatitis (a type of eczema) is the most common form.

Eczema: Skin inflammation (dermatitis) causing an itchy rash. Most often, it's due to an overactive immune system.

Psoriasis: An autoimmune condition that can cause a variety of skin rashes.

Silver, scaly plaques on the skin are the most common form Dandruff:

A scaly condition of the scalp may be caused by seborrheic dermatitis, psoriasis, or eczema.

Acne: The most common skin condition, acne affects over 85% of people at some time in life.

Cellulitis: Inflammation of the dermis and subcutaneous tissues, usually due to an infection. A red, warm, often painful skin rash generally results.

Skin abscess (boil or furuncle): A localized skin infection creates a collection of pus under the skin.

Some abscesses must be opened and drained by a doctor in order to be cured.

Rosacea: A chronic skin condition causing a red rash on the face. Rosacea may look like acne, and is poorly understood.

Warts: A virus infects the skin and causes the skin to grow excessively, creating a wart. Warts may be treated at home with chemicals, duct tape, or freezing, or removed by a physician.

Melanoma: The most dangerous type of skin cancer, melanoma results from sun damage and other causes. A skin biopsy can identify melanoma.

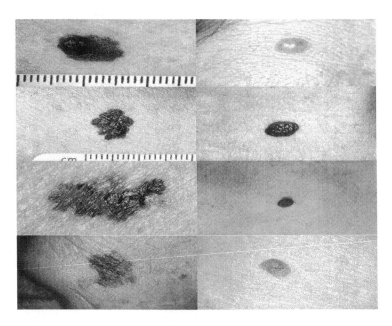

Melanoma

Basal cell carcinoma: The most common type of skin cancer.

Basal cell carcinoma is less dangerous than melanoma because it grows and spreads more slowly.

Seborrheic keratosis: A benign, often itchy growth that appears like a "stuck-on" wart. Seborrheic keratoses may be removed by a physician, if bothersome.

Actinic keratosis: A crusty or scaly bump that forms on sun-exposed skin.

Actinic keratoses can sometimes progress to cancer.

Squamous cell carcinoma: A common form of skin cancer, squamous cell carcinoma may begin as an ulcer that won't heal, or an abnormal growth. It usually develops in sun-exposed areas.

Herpes: The herpes viruses can cause periodic blisters or skin irritation around the lips or the genitals.

Hives: Raised, red, itchy patches on the skin that arise suddenly. Hives usually result from an allergic reaction.

Tinea versicolor: A benign fungal skin infection creates pale areas of low pigmentation on the skin.

Shingles (herpes zoster): Caused by the chickenpox virus, shingles is a painful rash on one side of the body. A new adult vaccine can prevent shingles in most people.

Scabies: Tiny mites that burrow into the skin cause scabies.

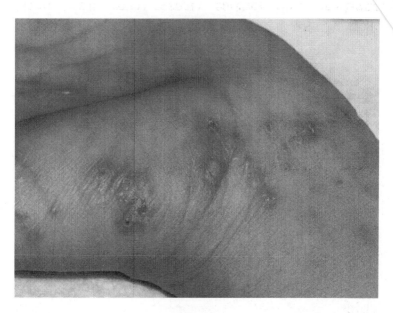

Scabies

An intensely itchy rash in the webs of the fingers, wrists, elbows, and buttocks is typical of scabies.

Ringworm: A fungal skin infection (also called tinea). The characteristic rings it creates are not due to worms.

A biopsy of the skin is a tiny piece of flesh that is removed for examination under a mi-

croscope in order to identify a skin condition.

Testing the skin detects any allergic reactions that are found and need to be treated.

Steroid medicines are given to reduce immune system activity. They may improve dermatitis.

Topical steroids are most often used on irritated skin.

Common anti-biotics are used to kill the bacteria which cause cellulite and other skin infections.

Medicines suppress the activity of the herpes virus, reducing its symptoms.

Topical creams can cure most fungal skin infections. Occasionally, oral medicines may be needed to be taken to cure fungal conditions.

Oral or topical medicines can block histamine, a substance that causes itching.

Most skin cancers must be removed by surgery.

Various drugs can modify the activity of the immune system, improving psoriasis or other forms of dermatitis. Emollients such as hydrating moisturizers are applied to very dry skin.

Dry skin is very likely to become irritated and itchy. These moisturizers can reduce symptoms of many dry skin conditions.

FUNGAL SKIN INFECTIONS

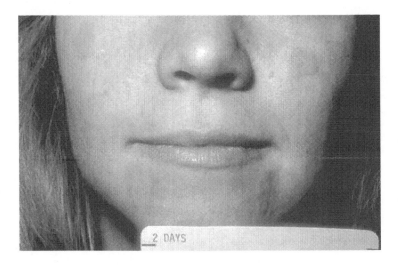

Fungal Infection

Fungal infections of the skin are very common and include athlete's foot, jock itch, ringworm, and yeast infections.

Ringworm

Worms do not cause ringworm. Most likely, this superficial skin infection, also known as tinea, is caused by fungi called dermatophytes.

Athlete's Foot

Athlete's foot is a common fungal infection and you don't have to be an athlete to get it. This annoying ailment occurs in boys, girls, men, and women of all ages.

Candidiasis (Yeast Infection)

Candidiasis is an infection caused by a group of yeast. There are more than 20 known species of Candida . These fungi live on all surfaces of our bodies.

Sporotrichosis

This fungus is related more closely to the mold on stale bread or the yeast used to brew beer than to bacteria that usually cause infections.

The mold is found on rose thorns, hay, sphagnum moss, twigs, and soil.

This type of infection is more common among gardeners who work with roses, moss, hay, and soil.

Fungal nail Infections occur when a fungus attacks a fingernail, a toenail, or the skin under the nail, called the nail bed.

VIRAL SKIN INFECTIONS

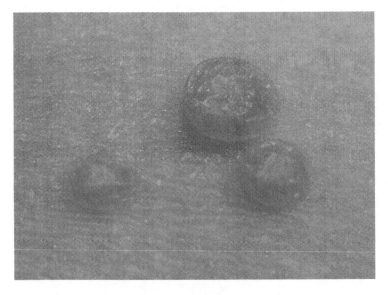

Viral Skin Infection

Molluscum Contagiosum

Molluscum contagiosum is a viral skin infection that causes either single or multiple raised, pearl-like bumps (papules) on the skin.

Shingles

Shingles (herpes zoster) results from a reactivation of the virus that also causes chickenpox.

Chicken pox

Chickenpox is a viral illness characterized by a very itchy red rash, is one of the most common infectious diseases of childhood.

A deeper look at symptoms.......

PSORIASIS

Psoriasis is a chronic skin condition caused by an overactive immune system.

Symptoms include flaking, inflammation, and thick, white, silvery, or red patches of skin. Psoriasis treatments include steroid creams, occlusion, light therapy and oral medications.

Skin problems are common for people of all ages. Whether you suffer with a rash, itchy skin, skin fungus or infection, skin bumps, or skin tags, there's a good treatment available for a variety of skin conditions.

If you have oily or dry skin, talk to your doctor about your particular skin type and learn the best methods to clean, treat, and protect your skin.

WHAT CAUSES ACNE?

Acne is a skin disease that's often misunderstood. Some people believe that it's contagious or is caused by dirt; both of these allegations are untrue.

There are a number of factors, like stress, that can contribute to acne.

Hormonal changes can contribute to acne, so women may be more susceptible during pregnancy and menopause. The severity of acne is determined by the scope and type of lesions. Moderate acne is characterized by inflammatory (papules, pustules, nodules) and noninflammatory (comedones) lesions.

Severe acne consists of numerous or extensive papules and pustules, as well as many nodules/cysts.

Why is this relevant to salon and spa treatments?

Anatomy and Physiology is of extreme importance to therapists' to perform treatments in the salon environment.

Beauty and Health Therapists receive in depth training in human Biology. Thorough knowledge of the human body is a priority.

A negligent Beauty Therapist's can be detrimental to the medical profession whereas worthy therapists rely on building a good rapport with physicians.

Therapists are duty bound to abide by the Professional Ethics at all times.

Minor contraindications

Cuts - an opening in the skin which is not healed.

Abrasion - a scraped area on the skin.

Scars - a mark left on the skin after an injury mainly a wound or surgery.

Moles -small congenital growth on the human skin, usually slightly raised and dark.

Hairs can grow out of moles such as pigmented nevus.

Cysts are non cancerous, closed pockets of tissue that can be filled with fluid, pus, or other type of material. Cysts are common on the skin and can appear anywhere. They feel like large peas under the surface of the skin. Cysts can develop as a result of infection, clogging of sebaceous glands (oil glands), or around foreign bodies, such as earrings.

Lumps and Bumps-There are a number of conditions that cause lumps and bumps to appear on the skin such as sebaceous, epidermal.

Melanoma - different types of tumors which are characterized by malignant growth of melanocytes.

Eczema - a skin inflammation with lesions that scale, crust or ooze out a serious fluid accompanied by intense itching and burning.

Dermatitis

Itching and redness is the basic symptoms of dermatitis, which has a variety of causes, including allergies.

Skin rash - change in texture and color of the skin in a particular area. Skin becomes itchy, bumpy, chapped, scaly and irritated.

Vitiligo - patches of non pigmented skin. The cause is unknown.

Impetigo - eruption of superficial pustules and yellow crusts on the face, a contagious bacterial infection.

Edema - inflammation of the skin which is noticeable and may be linked to phlebitis, thrombosis and other serious illnesses.

These occur in the circulatory system and must be diagnosed immediately.

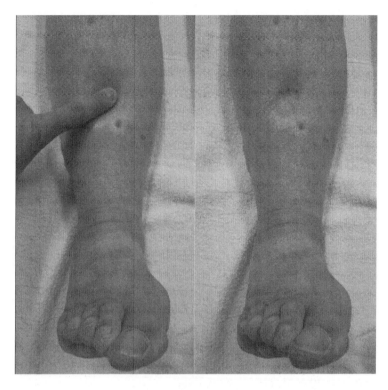

Edema

Telangastasia -ruptured capillaries of the skin seen on the face and body.

Varicose veins -veins are enlarged hey can be blue, red, or flesh-colored. They bulge out and appear twisted.

Burns -Burns are injuries caused by burning of the skin, The location of the lesion influences the severity of the burn.

Carbuncles - This occurs when there is Inflammation of the subcutaneous tissue resulting in sloughing up. They have a tendency to spread and though similar to a boil, are more serious in their effects.

Athlete's foot - a fungal skin infection that affects the feet found in the skin between the toes where itching, scaling, cracking and blisters characterize this condition.

Corns form small painful areas found on the toes. They are thick and painful.

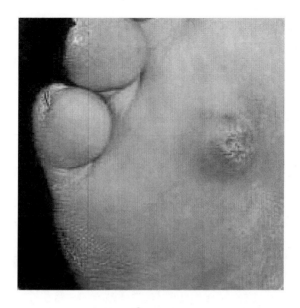

Corn

Callous is a roughened area of skin which has become relatively thick and hard in response to repeated friction, pressure, or any other irritation.

Ringworm is a common fungal infection of the skin, more common in males than in females; ringworm is characterized by patches of rough, reddened skin.

Raised eruptions usually form the circular pattern that gives the condition its name.

Ringworm may also be referred to as dermal infection deriving from the dermis lesions grow and the centers start to heal. The inflamed borders expand and spread the infection.

Contraindications to Manicure.

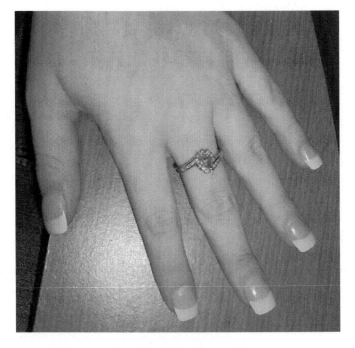

Manicure

Prior to commencing a manicure, the Therapist or Manicurist should check the hands and nails thoroughly for contraindications under a magnifier.

This is the only was to ensure that there are no warts on the hands, no fungal infections and to determine the state of the nails.

Are they brittle?

Do they need extra work?

Is the client a nail biter and has inflamed skin around her cuticles?

These clues which are observed by therapists will influence the judgment as to whether a client is suitable for treatment; in this case a simple manicure.

Visual contra-indications are easy to spot unlike major contra-indications.

They appear are on the surface of the skin and can be seen by the human eye.

Chapter 2

Which are the most important major contraindications to look out for?

Clients are asked about their medical history through a series of questions. These questions are compulsory.

Clients may well ask the therapist why these questions are of importance.

The answers the therapist relays to the client are a challenge for the therapist and will determine how knowledgeable the therapist is.

Clients with any of the following conditions must not be treated without a doctor's signed documents and the client's signature on the therapist's consultation card.

MAJOR MAJOR
CONTRA-INDICATIONS

Epilepsy

This is when there is abnormal or excessive activity of the neurons in the brain which cause unprovoked seizures that affect a person's movements and actions including levels of consciousness.

Epilepsy may be controlled with the help of medications. There is no permanent cure for Epilepsy.

CANCER

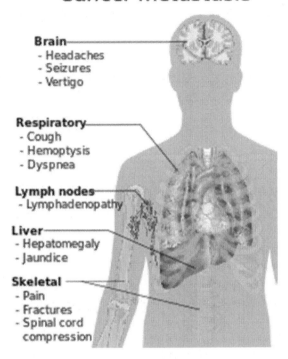

Common sites and symptoms of
Cancer metastasis

Brain
- Headaches
- Seizures
- Vertigo

Respiratory
- Cough
- Hemoptysis
- Dyspnea

Lymph nodes
- Lymphadenopathy

Liver
- Hepatomegaly
- Jaundice

Skeletal
- Pain
- Fractures
- Spinal cord compression

Metastasis of Cancer

Common cancers include skin, breast, colon, lung, prostate and lymphoma. Categories of Cancer fall into four stages, stage one being the least invasive and stage four is fatal.

Doctors will initiate treatment depending on the cancer by means of chemotherapy, radiation or major surgery.

People who have cancer take a lot of medication.

Chemotherapy

Chemotherapy is used to stop or slow down the growth of cancer cells. It does harm healthy cells that grow and divide quickly.

Many patients suffer from bad side effects following a chemotherapy treatment such as nausea and vomiting. Hair loss is common during Chemotherapy.

Radiation

Radiation is another form of treatment used to stop cancer cells from growing and dividing. It also has some negative side effect following treatment.

Knee replacement Surgery -A surgical procedure for severe knee damage which must be performed after severe knee injury to regain mobility in the knee joint.

Hip replacement Surgery

The diseased parts of the hip joints are removed during major surgery and replaced with new artificial parts to increase mobility and relieve pain.

Heart Problems

Heart problems are conditions of the cardiovascular system. There are many types of heart conditions such as heart murmurs, hole in the heart, heart attacks, enlarged heart.

Pacemakers are common in people who have suffered from heart problems and have had major surgery.

This is where therapists and doctors interact to assess whether treatments may be performed due to the increase of the circulation during treatment.

Blood Pressure

High blood pressure is dangerous and can lead to a heart attack or stroke.

Low blood pressure is also referred to as hypotension. Dizziness and fainting can be signs of low blood pressure.

Stress

When a person is over stressed, this can lead to many problems in the body. Stress is linked to heart attacks and stroke. Stress plays a major part in the deterioration of the body's health beginning with anxiety, depression, acidity and many other ailments.

Lung disease more than likely is related to smoking such as lung cancer. Pleurisy occurs when fluid gets into the lung and has to be removed immediately.

Kidney Diseases occur when bacteria travel up the body into the kidney causing infection.

Food for thought!

Diabetic clients are slow healers.

Longer time frames should be made between appointments.

Some types of diabetes can lead to kidney problems, patients having to undergo dialysis or removal of the pancreas.

Asthmatic clients are known to suffer from various allergies and are prone to shortage of breath. The client must have an inhaler at all times.

What is Hepatitis?

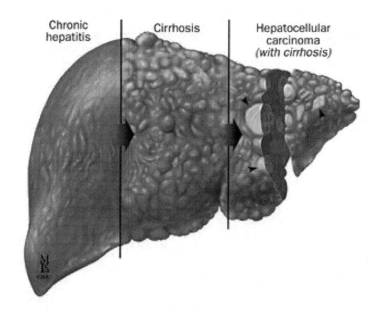

Chronic hepatitis Cirrhosis Hepatocellular carcinoma *(with cirrhosis)*

Hepatitis

Hepatitis occurs when injury to the liver results in inflammation and affects the cells in the liver.

A.I.D.S.

Human Immunodeficiency Virus (H.I.V.) also known as Acquired Immune Deficiency Syndrome (A.I.D.S.) The immune system fails to respond to any medication. This in turn makes the body more susceptible to serious infection and diseases; which eventually lead to cancer.

H.I.V. is fatal which means that there is no cure for this disease.

Beauty machines can interfere with metal pins or plates in the body. No electrical treatments should be performed.

In order to treat a client who has undergone major surgery which has been performed in the past five to seven years, it is necessary to have a signed doctor's certificate permitting treatment.

Following laser surgery, doctors can determine when a client is suitable for salon treatments.

Cosmetic surgery – Since the skin takes a long time to heal, a doctor's certificate is required.

Clients who have cosmetic procedures and chemical peels must inform their doctor before proceeding with beauty treatments.

Large Scars may be treated over the area following a two year period.

Small scars may be treated over the area following six to eight months.

What is Carpal Tunnel ?

The Carpal Tunnel is a narrow passageway of ligament and bones at the base of your hand. It contains nerves and tendons. Sometimes, thickening from irritated tendons or other swelling narrows the tunnel and causes the nerve to be compressed. Symptoms include numbness, sharp piercing pains.

Fibroids - heavy bleeding and abdominal pain may be linked to ovarian cancer and uterine diseases.

The symptoms are similar but must be checked by a Physician.

Lymphatic disorders occur when a weak immune system's white blood cells decrease and are unable to fight back the disease.

Circulation problems — recognition Phlebitis - very inflamed area in the legs such as the calf and the ankle area being swollen.

People with a slow metabolism tend to tire easily as the blood does not circulate well in the body.

Tumors

These fall into two categories malignant which means cancerous and benign with is non cancerous which only a Physician will be able to discover via various tests and recommend treatment.

Thrombosis, Phlebitis, Oedema are major contra-indications to the following treatments: Steam baths, massage and waxing.

Unexplained pain anywhere in the body could be dangerous if not diagnosed. Therapists will advise clients to pay a visit to a doctor to pinpoint the problem.

Recent tattoos or piercings

Precautions must be taken to ensure that the area has healed completely before treatment .

If the area inflames the area is probably infected.

Sunburn – The skin becomes very red due to over exposure of the skin to direct sunlight. Blistering of the skin is common.

Ultra– Violet Rays may be good in small doses but the truth is that sunburn can lead to early aging of the skin, burning of the skin and eventually to cancers of the skin.

Sun beds – Tanning beds with Ultra Violet. May be used safely maximum one hour per week, Over exposure will result in damaging the skin as sunburn.

Contraindication to Tinting :

- Cataracts
- Conjunctivitis
- Weeping eyes
- Contact lenses must be removed

Anxiety and Depression

Highly strung clients are more than likely to be claustrophobic, clay masks should never be applied during facial treatments.

Depression

Palpitations

Panic attacks

MUSCLE AND JOINT PAIN

Slipped disc

Arthritis

Back pain

Osteoporosis

Client Care

The manner in which a therapist treats a client from the moment she steps into the salon is crucial.

A therapist will ensure that client appointments are on time.

The therapist will help the client to get on and off the couch. They offer to remove their shoes and put them back on after treatment. Special attention is paid to clients to ensure that they are comfortable during treatment.

Chapter 3

Recreational Drugs

Obvious signs to look out for:

Observe the following:-

- Dilated pupils
- Avoids eye contact
- Slurred speech
- Lack of co-ordination
- Mood swings
- Irritability
- Angry outbursts
- Unusual hyperactivity
- Agitation
- Giddiness
- Appears lethargic or "spaced out"
- Fearful
- Anxious
- Paranoia
- Reeks of alcohol
- Glassy, red eyes

- Inappropriate laughter followed by sleepiness
- Contracted pupils
- Withdrawn
- Lacks concentration
- Euphoria
- Pupils are larger or smaller than usual
- Dry mouth and nose
- Watery eyes
- Secretions from the nose
- Rashes around the nose and mouth
- Headaches and nausea
- Appearance of intoxication
- Feeling drowsy
- Poor muscle control
- Bizarre or irrational behavior
- Hallucinations
- Needle marks
- Sweating
- Vomiting

Drugs have serious side effects!

Prescribed Medication

Precautions are taken and the client is asked to get a signed document by a general practitioner giving therapist's legal permission to perform the treatment.

This is then attached to the client record card. It may well be considered to be a guarantee allowing the Therapist to perform treatment.

Therapist stand to gain deep respect from doctors by demonstrating their professionalism.

A receptionist may be asked to act as a witness when signing the consultation card.

Record cards are divided for various treatments.

Manicures, Pedicure, Waxing and Makeup consultation codes are shorter.

All major contradictions are retained in consultations to perform facial and body treatments such as Galvanic, Faradic, Vacuum suction, Electrolysis and other electrical treatments.

ELECTRICITY – SAFETY

Clients should take note when safety regulations are not ignored.

Trailing wires.

Unused Sockets that are not covered for toddlers safety.

Faulty equipment.

Dirty equipment.

clean hands
save lives

hygiene

Rust on utensils or equipment.

Flickering light bulbs.

These are known signs of a negligent therapist at work.

GLOSSARY OF TERMS

Comedians are commonly known as blackheads.

Pustules – a small inflamed white spot that is filled with pus

People – a solid firm, hard painful elevation of skin with no visible fluid, varying in size from a pinhead to one centimeter.

Pupils can be brown, purple, pink or red in color.

Mainly found on oily skin types.

Vesicle– tiny as a pin, this type of spot is filled with fluid which leaves behind a yellow crust when dry.

Milia – deep seeded tiny white bumps which are hard and trapped beneath the skin. Milia can be found under the eye area.

Thread veins – ruptured vessels beneath the skin's surface mainly found on the face.

Telangiestasia – tiny ruptured blood vessels which may be otherwise referred to as spider veins.

Keloids – growth of extra scar tissue which darkens when exposed to the sun

Ephelides – also known as freckles is due to uneven distribution of melanin. Mainly found on fair skin. They may be reddish or brown in color and are flat to the skin's surface.

Skin Tags – small, unsightly elevated skin mainly found in elderly people on the neck and body.

Client's Name

Full Address

Telephone Number

Mobile Number

E-mail

Doctor's Name

Doctor's Mobile number

Contraindications

Major contraindications to treatment:

Epilepsy

Diabetes

Heart Conditions

Liver Disease

Kidney Disease

Circulatory disorders

Lymphatic disorders

Tumors

Cancers

Visual Contraindications on the Face

Hairy Moles

Carcinoma

Melanoma

Thread Veins

Eye Infections

Contact Lenses

Other .....

Client's Signature

Therapist's Signature

Witness Signature

Date

Notes:

Therapist enter additional notes for their perusal. These include previous treatments, dates performed and other additional information.

The client must then sign the Consultation Card. Proof of Identity can be verified via an Identity card or Passport.

Chapter 4

SKIN ANALYSIS

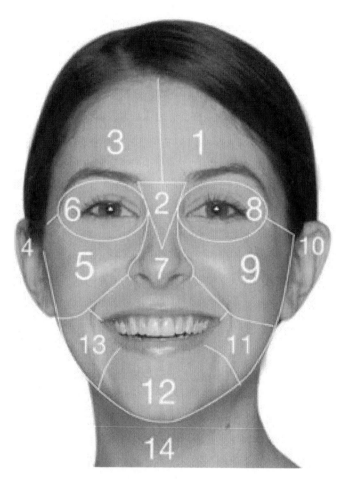

Skin Anlysis

A facial cleanse is followed by proper analysis of the skin before any treatment.

NORMAL SKIN

This skin has a healthy appearance

Few open pores are visible

Elasticity of the skin is good

The Punct Hydrogen (pH) is correct.

COMBINATION SKIN

Oily T-Zone (forehead, around the nose and chin area)

Comedians are present

Occasional papules

Pustules

Open pores

OILY SKIN

Skin looks shiny due to over secretion of the sebaceous gland

Dull, sallow complexion

Open pores

Papules

Pustules

What is Seborrhea?

Excessive discharge of sebum from the sebaceous glands

Recognition of Seborrhea

Pigmentation in certain areas (discoloration)

Shiny appearance

Pustules

Papules

Open pores

This is known as Seborrhoeic Skin.

SENSITIVE SKIN

Erythema

Closed pores

Thread veins

Milia

Dry/sensitive around the nose and mouth

Blotchy patches

DRY & DEHYDRATED SKIN

Fine lines are evident

Milia

Sensitive patches

Dry patches

Flaky areas

Dehydrated

MATURE SKIN

Very dry patches

Crow's feet around the eyes

Wrinkles

Flaking of the skin

Dehydrated with deep lines on the face and neck

ACNE VULGARIS

Acne Vulgaris is a common skin disorder

A disease of the sebaceous follicle, which primarily affects the face, chest, and back areas.

Normally occurs during puberty due to increased sebum production.

Acne Vulgaris may persist throughout adulthood

Inflammation is present

Lesions can be found on the skin

Pitting and scarring of the skin

Comedones

Papules

Pustules

Open pores define Acne Vulgaris

ACNE ROSACEA

A common disorder found in women between the ages of thirty to sixty.

Excessive flushing of the skin

Telangiectasia

Pustules

Papules

Erythema

Inflammation

General Home care advice

Use of a Sun block which blocks ultraviolet rays always avoid direct sunlight and wear a hat and sunglasses with a thick outer rim.

Avoid excessive smoking and drinking.

Eat healthy

Nutritious food

Drink plenty of water

Cleanse and tone the skin every day and never wear makeup to bed since chemicals are absorbed through the epidermis in minute quantities which over time can affect the internal organs.

Hydrating and nourishing of the skin using the correct emulsions.

Checking products used by clients and recommending the necessary amendments.

SLIMMING TREATMENTS

& Pregnancy & Breast Feeding

Pregnant   clients may not be treated on the abdomen. Electrical slimming machine on the abdomen this can cause a miscarriage.

Chapter 5

Liability

What can therapists be held liable for?

Losing credibility occurs when a therapist

makes a mistake.

We are only human and mistakes do happen.

Take an example of a minor incident such as tweezing extra hairs on the eyebrow.

Though not considered a serious error, the client will not be happy since the eyebrows will not be equal and there will be a slight gap.

When Beauticians, Beauty Therapists, Spa, Holistic Therapists, Massage Therapist lose credibility with the client and the outcome is loss of business and a bad reputation.

Should there be any misconduct by the Therapist, this is a breach of Professional Ethics and can lead to other problems.

Malpractice

Making a serious Professional error made by Therapists who did not follow protocol or therapists trying to cut down on their costs to increase their earnings.

Should a breach of Professional Ethics not be adhered to and negligence is discovered, at this point the Therapist suffers the consequences of those actions.

These matters are not taken lightly and will lead to being sued and taken to court with the possibility of losing your license to practice.

Therapists must be covered by professional indemnity insurance though will still be held accountable for causing traumatic injuries to the client.

Depending on the outcome of the inquest, if found guilty by a court inquest, the judge can prevent the therapist from the further practice.

Being negligent for having used faulty equipment on a client often result in a type of injury.

One example is using the Body Galvanic for Slimming Treatments.

Headline News

"Established Beauty Therapist sued for Negligence"!

Why was this Therapist sued?

This Therapist was very popular but was also money orientated and client care was poor.

The sponges which had been used on many Clients over time had become threadbare, allowing the electrical current to penetrate through the tiny pores of the sponges resulted in deep Galvanic burning of the skin.

As a result, the client had to undergo major skin surgery and skin grafting.

Professional Therapists know that one of the most important aspects is to cover the cut out sponges with the saline solution and place them correctly on the Galvanic pads before proceeding with treatment.

A Professional is also extremely aware of the importance of checking that all equipment and implements are in good condition.

Chapter 6

Personal and Public Hygiene

In a salon, spa environment or health care center, hygiene is of the utmost importance.

Personal hygiene

The Therapist should wear the uniform with pride.

Fob watch is allowed to be worn.

Jewelry should not be worn.

Hair must be tied back neatly.

Badges must be pinning them to the uniform.

Toothbrush and toothpaste

Hairbrush

Mouthwash

Sterilization in the Workspace

PUBLIC HYGIENE

Sterilize the hands after moving the magnifier around or touching any object.

Sterilize all instruments after each client and before commencing any treatment.

Wear gloves during waxing, pedicures and all treatments when required.

Use gloves which are comfortable and easy to work with.

Use of a face mask when performing certain treatments.

Clean towels and couch roll must be available for each client.

Blankets

Robes

Caps

Head Bands

Disposable Slippers

Disposable panties for bikini line waxing

Disposable mats for the floor beneath the couch

Keep your work area clean and tidy at all times.

The trolley must be spotless

Equipment must be in good working order

General cleaning

Floors should be spotless at all times

Glass windows must be clean

Vacuum carpets

Dust regularly

Clean waste paper baskets.

Use of a vacuum for carpet cleaning

Chapter 7

What must the First Aid Kit contain?

Antiseptic wipes

Antibacterial ointment

Bandage adhesive

Assorted fabric adhesive bandages

Gauze pads

Non stick sterile pads

Adhesive tape

Blister treatment

Pain relief tablets

After bite treatment lotion

Antihistamine to treat allergic reactions

Splinters

Fine point tweezers

Safety pins

Rolled gauze

FIRST AID MANUAL

Hand Sanitizer

Pure Aloe Vera Gel

Aspirin

Elastic wrap

Throat lozenges

Lubricating eye drops

Tablets (for diarrhea symptoms)

Poison Ivy treatment

Antifungal foot powder

Attendance to First Aid Courses once a year to keep up to date on new procedures.

Chapter 8

These   are courses where certificates of attendance are given to students.

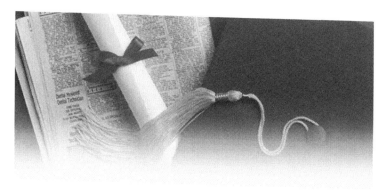

Nail Technician

Gellish Nails

Piercing

Tattooing

Mesotherapy

Aromatherapy

Reflexology

HD Brows

Threading

Micro Pigmentation

Skin Needling

Laser Treatments

Chemical Peels

Advanced Make-up Courses

Spa Training

Spa Management

Teaching

REFRESHER COURSES

Refresher Courses should be taken every
two years to ensure that changes in treatments are up to date.

Allergic substances are found in products. One example is ivy which is used in some brands of wax.

This may contain substances unsuitable for clients.

IVY is also found in Slimming Creams (Anti-Cellulite)

Skin and Cosmetic Ingredients which are known to be toxic:

Mineral oil

Propylene glycol

Polyethylene glycol

Isopropyl Alcohol

Sodium Lauryl Sulfate

Color Pigments

Fragrance

Alcohol

Lead

And many other toxic ingredients that are harmful to the body are found in a number of skin care products and cosmetics.

I recommend that clients use echo friendly skin care products , bio oils and aloe vera makeup which is widely available today.

Wishing you all a happy and safe spa to all the readers.

4318500R00050

Printed in Great Britain
by Amazon.co.uk, Ltd.,
Marston Gate.